This book belongs to

....

For Grace and all those other
"Very Special Ladies"

ISBN 978-1475 115895

Text © 2012 Nell Carswell

Illustrations © 2012 Sarah Merrigan

Text design © 2012 Pauline Haas

A Very Special Lady

Written by Nell Carswell

Illustrated by Sarah Merrigan

"Harriet, darling, do you have your pyjamas on?"

"Yes, Mummy."

"Good girl, shall we go and clean your teeth then before Daddy reads you a bedtime story?"

"OK, Mummy."

"What story shall we read tonight, darling?"

"Daddy, could you read me that special story?"

"Which story is that, darling?"

"You know Daddy, that special story about that very special lady."

"Certainly, Darling."

Once a pot a time ...

A long time ago, a very long time ago,
your Mummy and Daddy tried to have a baby.

They tried and tried and tried and tried
and kept on trying.

But they didn't have a baby.

All the time they were trying they would get cross and sad and grumpy and sometimes even mad.

They were never really, really happy.

Eventually, Mummy and Daddy went to see a doctor.

The doctor said we will have to do some tests
on Mummy and Daddy.

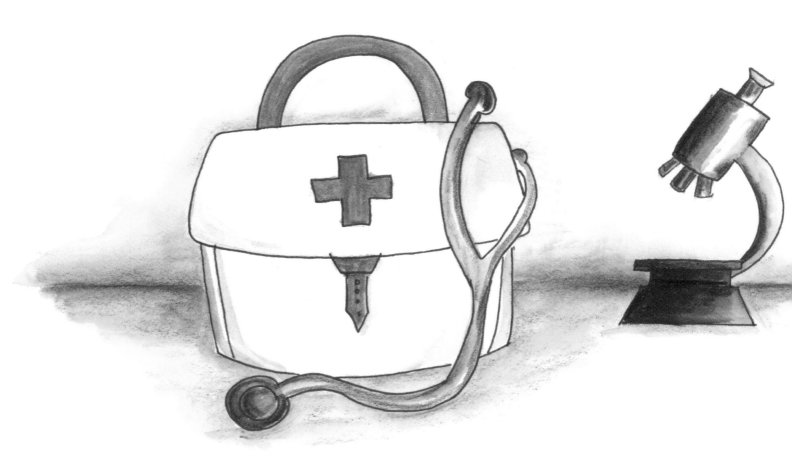

So Mummy and Daddy had tests

and tests and more tests.

After all these tests Mummy and Daddy went back
to see the doctor.

The doctor said that the only way they could have
a baby was if they could find a very special lady.

So Mummy and Daddy went off to find this very special lady.

Mummy and Daddy searched and searched
and kept on searching.

They searched everywhere.

They searched high
and low, near and far, in the
cities and over the seas.

Then one day they found her. Her name was Grace.

She was the very special lady Mummy and Daddy needed to help them have a baby.

Why did they need the very special lady, you may ask?

Well, what they actually needed was the very special lady's eggs so the doctor could put them together with a special bit of Daddy.

The doctor then put this tiny, tiny, tiny bundle into Mummy's tummy.

When the doctor had done this, the very special lady went home with her fingers crossed and Mummy and Daddy waited ...

... and waited and ... waited.

Over a long time Mummy's tummy got bigger
and bigger and bigger and bigger.

The special bundle in Mummy's tummy was growing …

… and growing
and growing.

Eventually, the baby was too big for Mummy's tummy.

So Mummy went to the hospital and, with the help of the doctor and nurses, out came the most beautiful little baby.

She was perfect in every way.

Mummy and Daddy took the little baby home.

The first thing they did was to tell all their friends and family
— and of course the VERY special lady —
that a most beautiful little baby girl had arrived.

Do you know the name of that very special little baby?

Her Mummy and Daddy named her Harriet.

So that is the story of the very special lady who helped Mummy and Daddy have a very special little girl.

And, do you know what?

Mummy and Daddy have not stopped smiling.